SPOONFULS
OF WISDOM

with a new epilogue by
Nathan Tolzmann and Matt Bergstrom

Book One in the Fiberglass Philosophers Series

©2015 Wurlington Press, Chicago IL
First Edition–1990
Second Edition—1991
Third Edition—2001
Fourth Edition—2015

ISBN 978-1-329-84674-6

Contents

Introduction

When one thinks of the sages of modern life, the first name that often springs to mind is that of Happy Chef. The Chef's teachings have changed so many lives and certainly affected every human. How can one have heard his thoughtful voice and not be struck by the wisdom capable of transcending age, racial, economic, social, geographical, sexual preference and religious boundaries? His genius and subtlety have often been compared to that of Plato and Confucious. How was Happy Chef able to achieve such greatness?

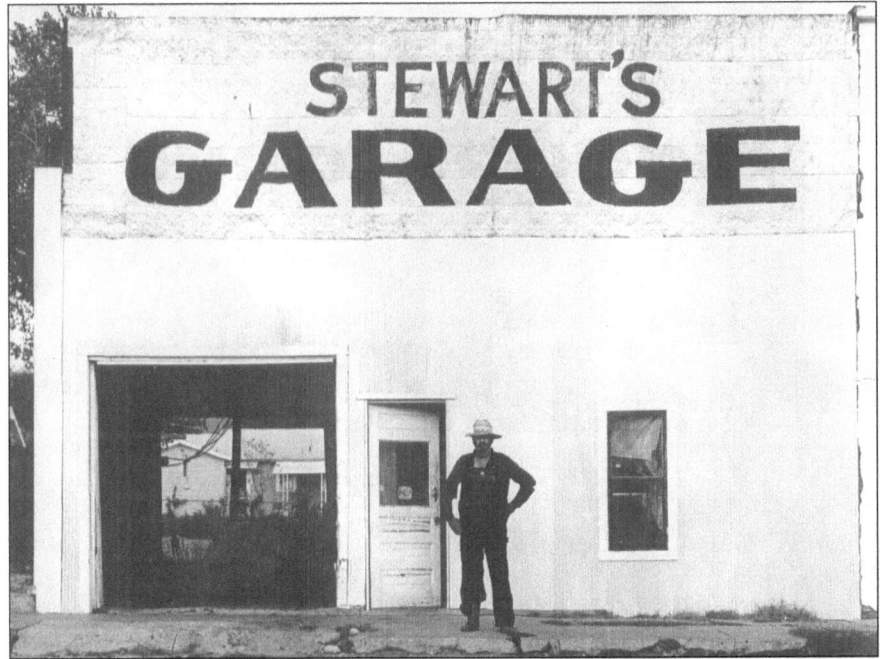

The birthplace of Happy Chef

Little is known about young Happy's childhood or adolescence aside from his early experiences with gasoline engines. Happy's two older brothers Charles and Edward were well known on the jalopy-racing circuit, while Happy fast became the best grease monkey on the track. After the brothers' tragic accident, Happy swore off the wrench and oil can and took up poetry to overcome his grief. His skill with the pen quickly improved and at the age of twelve he had won his first contest, the *Saturday Evening Post* Young Writer's Competition. Happy gave the $1.20 to Mr. and Mrs. Chef for their anniversary.

Mr. and Mrs. Myron B. Chef

We next hear of Happy during his student years at Middlebury. Like so many young men of his generation, Happy had a difficult time settling into an occupation. For a brief period he was an elevator operator, but the constant up and down motion caused him to develop an inner ear disorder which forced him to seek other employment. Happy then decided to enter the police academy. Happy's mother was fearful for his safety, however, so he withdrew from the academy. Discouraged, he again set out to find his calling. A brief stint as a shoe salesman left him despondent and starved for spiritual satisfaction. His Professor Bilkin recalls, "he was hungry,

hungry for knowledge." Happy's appetite led him to leave school after his junior year to seek out Jean-Paul Claude, the French philosopher/ nutritionist.

Jean-Paul, living at that time at a monastery in the Pyrenees, was so impressed by young Happy that he immediately agreed to take him in as an apprentice. Under Claude's attentive eye, Happy

Middlebury Razorbacks (Happy far right)

developed an astounding skill in the preparation of food and the mind. After his mentor's death, Happy was still not satiated. He was lead to the country of Bhutan in the Himalayas. Here he learned the simple art of cooking rice as a method towards enlightenment. The story of the peacock's tail (Book 3:5) is an example of the simplicity and elegance that characterizes Happy's Zen influence of that time. He spent his days in Bhutan turning prayer wheels and perfecting his recipes. After a year, Happy returned to his homeland to spread his revolutionary philosophy. He soon opened his first restaurant, which was an immediate success. The American public, starving for the mental nourishment Happy Chef could provide, enabled him to open a dozen more stores within eighteen months. And the people's support shows no sign of slowing yet.

While Happy Chef is known to have kept extensive diaries of his daily thoughts, sadly the only verses still remaining from that great mind are the twenty-eight printed in this volume. Until recently it was widely believed that there were only nineteen. In fact the nine verses that make up Book Four were not present in the previous edition of this book. The discovery of these additional verses has been greeted by much jubilation and perhaps an equal amount of skepticism. Are these authentic teachings of the Happy Chef, or did the prophet stop speaking long ago? The authors have chosen to embrace Book Four as part of the canon. Still, despite these newly found proverbs, students of Happy Chef have had to reconcile themselves to the fact that so little is left of his wisdom. Just what did the master mean by these few words?

Many scholars have theorized on the meanings of the Chef's enigmatic proverbs, but there is as of yet little consensus. We will try to relate to the reader the more widely accepted interpretations. As the late theologian Wilford H. Thomason once said, "Happy Chef's words will be misinterpreted, misunderstood and will mystify, but their importance will never be denied."

For the beginning student of the Great Chef, Happy's proverbs offer the entrance to an entire cuisine of truth and inner peace. When the hungry passerby hears the words of the Happy Chef and decides to become a little chef, he or she begins to follow the path to enlightenment and wisdom. Enlightenment is never fully found, however, for even the Great Chef, instead of being finished, is only "nearly an adult." (Book 4:4) Despite his great wisdom, he is far from full.

In addition, Happy says "being an adult is when you stop growing on each end and start growing in the middle" (Book 4:4). This is generally agreed to mean that the search for truth is not a search for objects outside the self, but for truths known by the self but perhaps forgotten. True wisdom is something we must search for inside the self, like the satisfaction of eating a stack of buttermilk pancakes. As Happy says, "it isn't the things you don't know that get you into trouble, it's the things you know for sure that turn out to be wrong"

Happy Chef and Pope John XXIII greet the people of Venice

(Book 4:5). The trust we previously put in concepts and things out-side ourselves must be left behind to follow truth.

Even the Great Chef himself must be left behind if we are to become true little chefs. Although some believe him to be divine (a controversy rooted entirely in Book 2:6: "Some people thought I was more than just the Happy Chef. Its true!"), the authors, how-ever, believe Happy would want the little chefs to pursue their own inner peace, as evidenced by his statement "I guess I'll have to wait out here for you and I'll see you when you come out" (Book 3:2). In the end the little chef must rely only on his or her own judgement.

In a recent essay, the eminent Happy Chef theorist Anna R. C. Trammel examines the influence of the Chef's Bhutan period on his later philosophy. This influence is particularly evidenced in his view of the relationship between the mind and body. Happy believed there to be no distinct separation between the two. In Book 3:3 he states "I had a ringing in my ears all day, but it went away when I answered the telephone. Uh-huh-huh..." A sensation perceived by the mind can become a sensation perceived by the body and vice versa. To Happy there was a direct relationship between the physi-cal and mental worlds — they were made of the same ingredients.

This explains Happy's connection of food and philosophy. He says "you have to take care of your body, because, where would you be without it?" (Book 2:3). The mind and the body are important to the existence of little chefs. Happy's theories about the cultivation of food are not just a metaphor for the cultivation of the mind—they are the process by which the mind is prepared and consumed by wisdom.

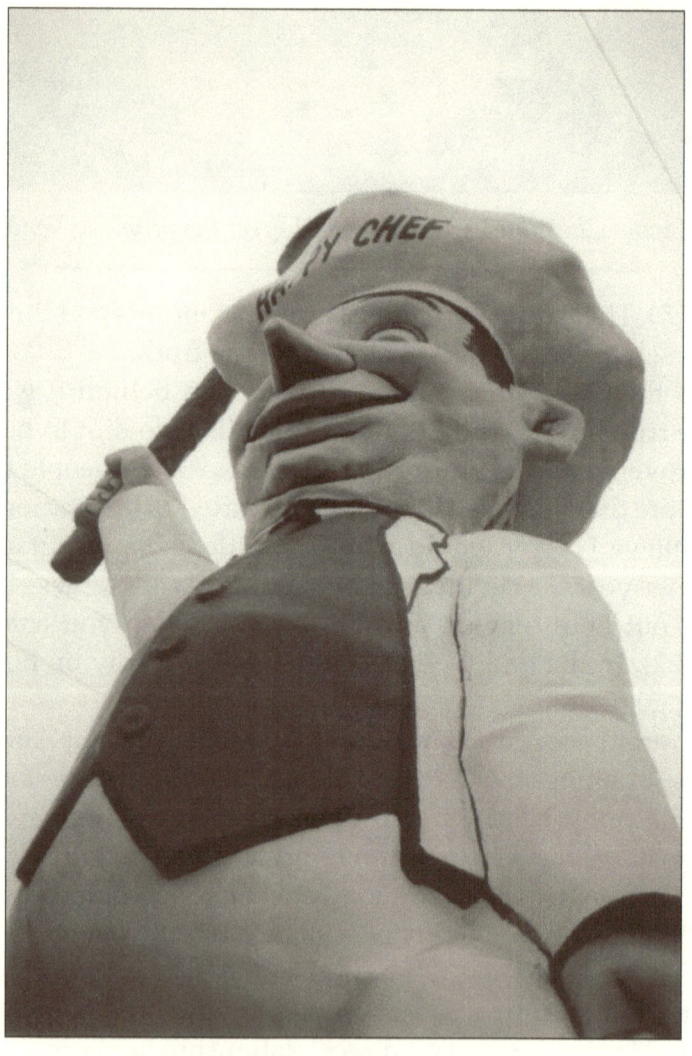

"I Should Be Called Skyscraper"

The recent discovery of the nine proverbs of Book 4 has caused much excitement and activity among Happy Chef scholars. It may be years before we understand the ramifications of these new verses. Through years of study, comparison and intense scrutiny, the world will gain a greater understanding of the wisdom of the Happy Chef. In the meantime, we have these few verses to read and take to heart.

Book 1

---

[1]Some folks call me crystal because I'm always on the watch and some folks call me clock because I always have the time, the time to talk to nice folks like you.

Georgie Jessel, Rosalind Russel, Happy Chef, Groucho Marx, Frank Sinatra, Irving Berlin, Dinah Shore, and Dean Martin

---

[2]A friend of mine has a fine-toothed comb. He's the only person I know who combs his teeth. Uhah.

[3]Boy, oh boy, kids, you know, during the week I really look

forward to the weekends because on the weekends more and more nice people like you come and see me—I really like that!

[4]A friend of mine just came by and told me that the reason we have laps is that so more than one person can sit on a chair at a s-[sic], at any one time. Do you think that's so?

[5]Do you know that the dachshund is a very, very brave little dog? It must be.[a]

[6]Someone once told me that the wolf would be at my door so I put a trap on the porch, but all I caught was the mailman. I guess you can't win them all.

[7]Hey all you little chefs, may I give you a piece of advice? When it's raining cats and dogs outside, be sure not to fall into a poodle! Uh heh. See ya'.

Happy Chef, Nikolai Shvernik, Nikita Krushchev, Georgi Dimitriov, Joseph Stalin, Vyacheslav Molotov, Artem Mikoyan, Vlas Chubar

---

[a]On other occasions, Happy Chef followed this statement with: "It has so much backbone. Uheh."

Book 2

[1]Hi! Did you know that a foreign language to a cat would be WOOF! WOOF! Don't you think so? Try barking at your cat sometime and see if he understands. And say "Hi" for me while you're at it. Okay?

Touring Southeast Asia

²Do you know what a fossil is? A fossil is something dug up by an archeologist. If a dog dug them up, we would probably just call them bones. I guess that's the way it goes.

³To be big and strong like me you have to eat the proper foods like the ones you get at the Happy Chef. You have to take care of your body, because—where would you be without it? Uh huh ha.

⁴When you get inside, if you notice that the ice is gone from your glass of water, don't worry, sometimes the water gets hungry and eats the ice. It happens all the time.

⁵Tell your daddy that if he orders soup, he better trim his moustache, because it might be a strain. Did you like that joke?

⁶Some people thought I was more than just the Happy Chef. It's true! Some people thought I should be called encyclopædia, because I'm so full of information. What do you think?

Book 3

¹I've been told that I should be called skyscraper because I'm so tall but I think it's because I'm so full of stories. Ha ha.

Happy Chef on Hollywood Squares

²Would you like to come inside with me? Oops, I can't fit through the door. I guess I'll have to wait out here for you and I'll see you when you come out, Okay?

³Hi little chefs! I had a ringing in my ears all day, but it went away when I answered the telephone. Uh-huh-huh...

[4]Did you know that heat makes everything get bigger and cold makes everything get smaller? Well, everything if you forget about ice cubes. See you later.

[5]Did I ever tell you the story about the peacock? Oh, let me tell you, it was a beautiful tale. Did you like that one? Uheh.

The world's largest ball of twine

---

[6]You know, a little chef like you once told me that he didn't like to go to school. When I asked why he didn't, he told me that it wasn't the school that he didn't like, it was the principle of the thing.

Book 4

¹Hi, when I eat I have to use a shovel for a spoon and a pitchfork for a fork, but we have smaller silverware for you.

²One of the other little chefs told me that the first law that was passed when our country was new was the law of gravity which made it against the law to fly around with- out an airplane, but I don't believe that, do you?

³There's something I don't understand that maybe you can help me with. How come in America economy sizes are big in bars of soap and small in cars? I just don't get it.

⁴Did you notice that I'm starting to get a little chubby? That's because I'm nearly an adult. Being an adult is when you stop growing on each end and start growing in the middle.

Ghandi leads group over catwalk (Happy in background)

[5]Y'know, I was just thinking it isn't the things you don't know that get you into trouble, it's the things that you know for sure that turn out to be wrong. See you later.

[6]Did you know that back in the horse and buggy days there weren't as many accidents, because then the driver had some help if he got in trouble. Drive carefully when you leave, Okay?

[7]You know, before I became the Happy Chef I tried a lot of other jobs. I used to be an elevator operator, but I quit because that job had too many ups and downs.

[8]I wanted to be a policeman once, but my mother wouldn't let me cross the street alone, so I had to give that up, but I like what I'm doing now.

[9]I wanted to be a shoe salesman, but I felt like such a heel, and I had no sole. So, I am here so I could meet all of you.

Appendix

Hey, little chefs! How often have you been to see the Happy Chef? Check off each visit.

Minnesota
☐ ~~Austin~~ *closed*
☐ ~~Barnum~~ *closed*
☐ ~~Fairmont~~ *closed*
☐ ~~Faribault~~ *closed*
☐ ~~Hutchinson~~ *closed*
☐ ~~Mankato~~ *closed*
☐ North Mankato
☐ ~~Marshall~~ *closed*
☐ ~~Northfield~~ *closed*
☐ ~~Owatonna~~ *closed*
☐ ~~Plymouth~~ *closed*
☐ ~~Rogers~~ *closed*
☐ ~~Roseville~~ *closed*
☐ ~~St. Cloud~~ *closed*
☐ ~~Shakopee~~ *closed*
☐ ~~Waseca~~ *closed*
☐ ~~Willmar~~ *closed*
☐ ~~Windom~~ *closed*
☐ ~~Winona~~ *closed*
☐ ~~Worthington~~ *closed*

Iowa
☐ ~~Adair~~ *closed*
☐ ~~Algona~~ *closed*
☐ ~~Ames~~ *closed*
☐ ~~Cedar Falls~~ *closed*
☐☐ ~~Cedar Rapids~~ (2) *closed*
☐ ~~Cherokee~~ *closed*
☐ ~~Clear Lake~~ *closed*
☐ ~~Council Bluffs~~ *closed*
☐ ~~Creston~~ *closed*
☐ ~~Dubuque~~ *closed*
☐ ~~Fort Dodge~~ *closed*

Iowa (continued)
☐ ~~Missouri Valley~~ *closed*
☐ ~~Onawa~~ *closed*
☐ ~~Oskaloosa~~ *closed*
☐ ~~Story City~~ *closed*
☐ ~~Waterloo~~ *closed*
☐ ~~West Des Moines~~ *closed*

Kansas
☐ ~~McPherson~~ *closed*

Nebraska
☐ ~~Columbus~~ *closed*
☐ ~~Greenwood~~ *closed*
☐ ~~Lincoln~~ *closed*
☐ ~~West Omaha~~ *closed*

North Dakota
☐ ~~Fargo~~ *closed*

South Dakota
☐ ~~Huron~~ *closed*
☐ ~~Kadoka~~ *closed*
☐☐ ~~Mitchell~~ (2) *closed*
☐ ~~Pierre~~ *closed*
☐☐ ~~Rapid City~~ (2) *closed*
☐ ~~Sioux Falls~~ *closed*
☐ ~~Yankton~~ *closed*

Wisconsin
☐ ~~La Crosse~~ *closed*
☐ ~~Mauston~~ *closed*
☐ ~~Sparta~~ *closed*

Afterword

The original publication of *Spoonfuls of Wisdom* in 1990 revolutionized the popular knowledge of fiberglass philosophers. The book remains a landmark of Happy Chef scholarship, as well as providing a much-needed paperback reference for travellers and those on the go. Previous works in the field were thick and weighty tomes both in volume and tone, which all too often induced sleepiness, a temptation to read while prone on the couch, and the inevitable collapse of the heavy book onto the readers nose. Tragically, several devoted readers were literally smothered by Happy's words in the mid 1980s.

But the publication of the original slim-sized edition of *Spoonfuls of Wisdom* brought a new lightness to the field and enlivened and enlightened the lives of many new recruits to the way of the Great Chef. It also brought a slim-sized fame and fortune to its authors Tolzmann and Bergstrom. The authors accepted the many laurels and accolades piled upon their heads with grace and a few chuckles in the spirit of Happy himself, while enjoying complimentary refills of coffee and other perks that accompanied their newfound success.

Hoping for a best-seller

The authors appear at a book signing at the Book Mark

A highlight of the *Spoonfuls of Wisdom* promotional tour was a book signing at the Gustavus Adolphus College bookstore "The Book Mark," where elusive Gustavus president John Kendall arrived for a treasured signed copy of the book. Many students and faculty as well turned from their fast food afflictions and rededicated themselves to the wholesome ingredients of Happy Chef.

All early editions of the book included a mysterious phrase on the copyright page: "All proceeds go to the Graceland Pilgrimage Fund." The brisk sales of the original edition were indeed deposited in a fund toward a future pilgrimage to Elvis Presley's Graceland estate.

Production costs for the first edition were low, thanks in part to an illicit copy of the key to the English department copy room, so even at the bargain price of 99¢ per copy, the Graceland Pilgrimage fund accrued a minor nest egg, enough to buy a tank or two of gas and the tickets required to enter Elvis' hallowed home.

In the fall of 1990, over the Thanksgiving holiday, the authors along with friend Suzanne Phelps set off in an orange AMC Gremlin toward the gold-spangled halls of Graceland, with a handmade Thanksgiving greeting card for Elvis himself, signed by passersby and other well-wishers met along the road. A middle-aged woman, the manager of a campground in Keokuk, Iowa, signed the card:

"Been yours a long time."

South across the prairies, the pilgrims made a stop at the Surf Ballroom to pay respects to the memorial for the last show of The Big Bopper, Ritchie Valens and Buddy Holly.

In Des Moines, a street preacher named Pastor John approached with offers of help. He was sure the travelers were headed for danger. He himself had been down that road: not towards Graceland, but towards danger. "I don't know why I never got a tattoo. So many guys I know who find the Lord regret their tattoos, but I never got one. I think maybe I should preach a sermon about that one day." He blessed the journey to smooth the asphalt waters ahead. The travelers, before heading back out on the road into the night, promised that they would stop by the mission on their return north.

In Hannibal, Missouri, that other Midwestern fiberglass philosopher, Mark Twain, offered his own homespun wisdom, and the guidance of the Mississippi River downstream. Finding themselves far beyond the fringes of Happy Chef's familiar territory the hungry travelers were forced to take their Thanksgiving meal at a Denny's restaurant outside St. Louis. Spirits were lowered by the meager fare and the insipid Muzak soundtrack, and they found no

Pastor John blesses the travelers

friendly chef standing outside the door to help lift them again.

The three pilgrims' morale greatly improved upon seeing the lights of Memphis at last. Graceland would not be open until the morning so they set up camp and tried to sleep, restless with anticipation. Early the next day, fueled by the red-eye gravy at a country diner on the edge of town, they entered the house, where a pre-recorded voice of Elvis himself welcomed them and asked them to "walk a mile in his shoes" to learn of the King's life and legacy.

Like the story of the peacock (Book 3:5), it was a beautiful tale, an American trilogy of youthful promise, over-reach and faltering, followed by a hard-won comeback. The many rooms of the King's mansion itself were just an empty memorial to a man who had strutted his brief time on a stage and had now left the building. The

Towering giant of American literature

pilgrims' thoughts returned again to the Happy Chef. The parallels between the two giant's lives were many, but how would the chef's story end? And how would he be memorialized? The travelers laid the Thanksgiving greeting card in tribute and thanks upon Elvis' grave, and realized they had reached the pinnacle of their journey.

Their quest completed, the trio explored other local points of interest: The Peabody Hotel with its elevator-riding waterfowl, the Memphis Police Museum, and Beale Street. While admiring a monumental bronze of Elvis on Beale Street (Book 3:2), an inebriated carpet cleaner approached. He had been in the homes of many Memphians of all creeds, colors, and kinds. "Every home in Memphis has three framed pictures," he declared, "Jesus, J.F.K. and Elvis," before stumbling off towards a night of revelry, leaving the travelers wondering if someday a fourth portrait could be added to that proverbial living room: The Happy Chef.

With minds and spirits full, it was time to head back to the snowy north and home. Remembering their promise to Pastor John they exited the highway in Des Moines and found the address he'd given them. Entering a shabby mission building they found

Laying the card on Elvis' grave

themselves in a "men only" day room. A snaggletoothed man with dented forehead sitting at a metal desk grunted: "Can I help you?" "We're looking for Pastor John." "Who? There ain't no Pastor John here." Finally one of the men sitting watching television twisted around and asked, "Who they lookin' for?" "Someone named Pastor John." "Do they mean Fat John?"

Fat John was overjoyed to see the pilgrims again, and surprised that they'd survived the journey. Presuming they must be famished from their tribulations, he pressed upon them a sack of bologna sandwiches (Book 2:3), which they would only accept in exchange for a copy of *Spoonfuls of Wisdom* they pressed into his hand. Behind his beard, perhaps he did bear some resemblance to the great chef, and he certainly did seem happy. After a few tales of his prodigal youth, Pastor John bid adieu to the pilgrims and they headed back to the highway.

The events of the journey had given the travelers much to discuss and they discussed it all as they hurtled down the road. They'd met so many fascinating people in the past few days. Were all these

Graceland or Bust

fellow pilgrims not just ingredients in a great American bean soup, stirred by some master chef in that great roadside diner on high? Would all the restless stirring and nighttime roadtrips and rolling wheels of history cease turning when the dish was finished? Were Elvis and Happy Chef and all threads of American culture bound together like the endless ribbons of asphalt connecting all corners of our land? Lost in the abstract world of the mind, they failed to notice the state of the gas gauge in the physical world. Discussion stopped and the car did too.

Before the stranded motorists even had a chance to begin worrying about their predicament a sedan pulled onto the shoulder behind them. The elderly couple on their way home from a long journey themselves were more than happy to lend a helping hand to fellow travelers.

It was as if the Happy Chef himself had sent a miracle from the horse and buggy days: "The driver had some help if he got in trouble." (Book 4:6) The good Samaritans helped the travelers fill their empty gas tank and they heeded the Chef's advice to, "Drive carefully when you leave, okay?"

Epilogue

The achievement of an important milestone inevitably leads one to reflection. This is true even if the achievement is merely the passage of time (Book 1:1). What pithy and humorous words would the Happy Chef have to bless the authors of *Spoonfuls of Wisdom* upon returning to a discussion of his great works on the 25th anniversary of that book's original publication?

Sadly we have no way of knowing the master's feelings on the subject, as he has fallen silent. Ever since the discovery of the Apocryphal Teachings (Book 4, included in the second edition of this book), fans have pleaded for further instruction from the great chef but he has refused all interviews and commentary on today's world.

Due to the deleterious effects of so many Midwestern winters standing sentinel outside his namesake restaurants, the fiberglass

Happy Chef at the original North Mankato location

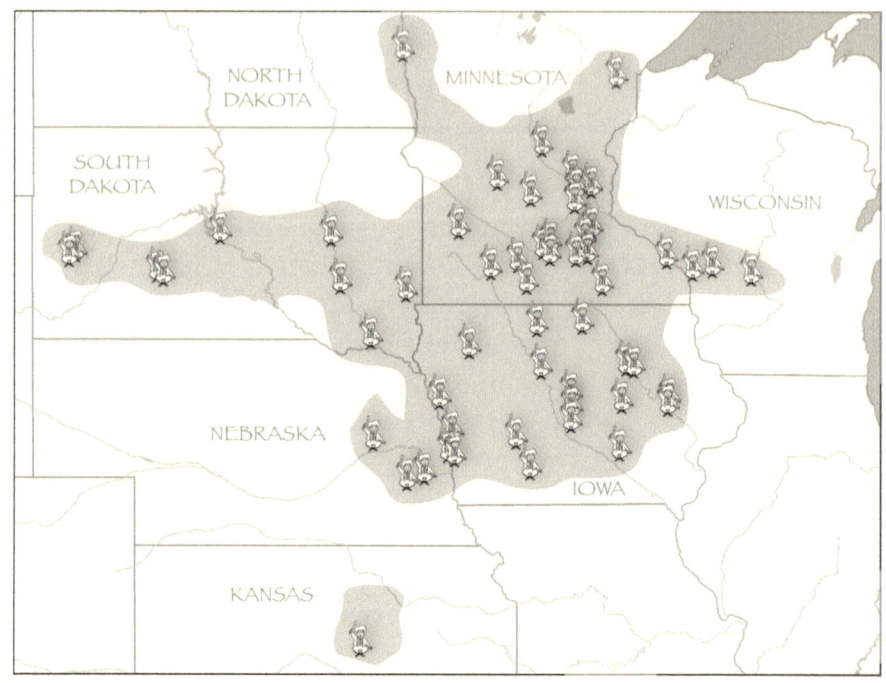

Greatest extent of the Happy Chef Empire

giant ceased speaking not long after the original publication of *Spoonfuls of Wisdom* in 1990. Even then, scholars knew that Happy's words were coming from an ancient current of deep wisdom, but they had no idea just how aged and corroded that wiring within him was.

Today is a far different world from the one twenty-five years ago when we discovered the Great Chef beckoning to us from the shoulder of a bleak thoroughfare outside Mankato, Minnesota. It was our first contact with Happy Chef's great empire of 56 restaurants purveying his unique brand of food and philosophy for a hungry and seeking world. Most of these blessed establishments were located alongside busy highways to feed and comfort the lonely travelers and forsaken wanderers of life.

It was impossible for Happy to be everywhere at once, and yet he made every effort to be as present as often and at as many locations as was physically possible. Then again, practical physicality rarely hindered his movements as he was able to seemingly cover long distances between establishments giving the appearance of omnipresence. No doubt his impressive size and powerful quadriceps enabled him to make these great leaps across time and space to personally speak to even the smallest chefs of his realm.

Under the reign of his great spoon lifted high, residents and visitors to the small towns of the upper Midwest enriched their minds and middles on the delicious buttery aroma of Happy's wise waffle fries, peaceful pancakes and graceful grilled burgers.

And yet over the years, Happy's tours of his territory seemed less frequent. Expectant highway travellers looking for a boon of his words found his towering form missing. Visitors might still fill their bellies, but not their minds, as the great chef and his wisdom were too often absent.

Then, one by one, the restaurants began to close their doors, to be converted to Mexican eateries and sports bars. Places of a certain spirit but entirely lacking in Happy's jovial chortle, leaving his followers feeling alone in the wilderness and stranded by the side of a lonely road.

Ruins of the Great American 24-Hour Breakfast

For devotees of His Chefness, the closing of these pilgrimage sites was a great loss. What a sense of frustration and grief for the spiritual tourist seeking to check off the full list of restaurants in the back of the original edition of *Spoonfuls of Wisdom*, upon discovering that their collection would be forever and impossibly incomplete?

For other travellers, the rare joy of coming upon Happy standing at his restaurant outpost while on a road trip would be tempered by disappointment at the great statue's loss of words. Why had the Happy Chef stopped talking? Was he silent because his restaurants were steadily disappearing, or were the restaurants disappearing because he refused to speak?

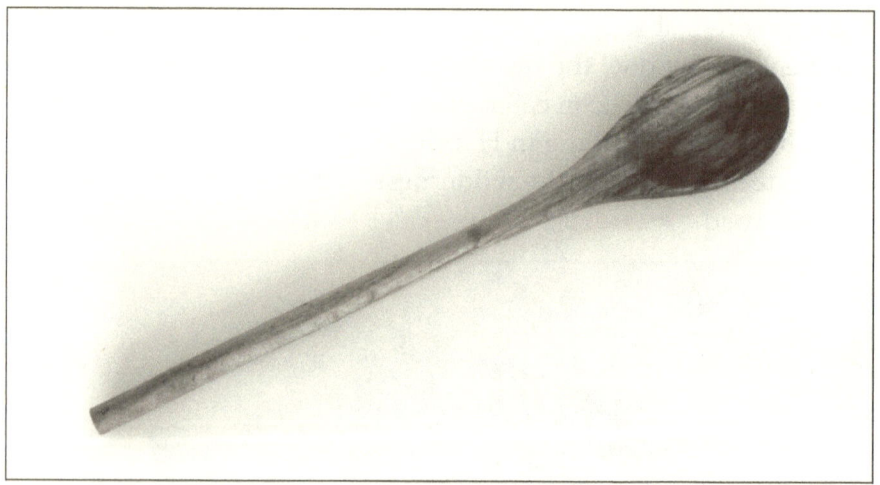

Spoon of wisdom: a treasured relic of the jolly Chef

One by one the many Happy Chef restaurants closed their doors throughout the 2000s and 2010s. Managers blamed changing trends in the hospitality industry. "Young people are more interested in a bar and grill concept," said Chad Cubbage, a Cedar Falls food service consultant. But where will today's youth find a hearty 24-hour breakfast, a combo skillet dinner, and home-cooked philosophical wisdom? These endangered Midwestern foodways and homespun insight represent a lost heritage, only one of which can be preserved in this book.

By 2015, one lone Happy Chef restaurant remained of the chain, the original location which opened in 1963. It was this very same place where we first met the Great Chef many years ago and first heard his humble and inspiring voice. The restaurant is currently for sale, and its days appear numbered.

How swiftly the passing decades have left a once-great philosophical empire in ruins! It is sad to see the mute Chef making his lonely stand outside his last surviving restaurant, but it is our hope that his written words will live on and continue to enlighten new generations long after the kitchen of that last restaurant closes. When the last cinnamon roll has gone stale and the last patty melt has moldered away, Happy's ideas will still live on in our hearts.

Perhaps this new volume can reach past shallow nostalgia into a deeper appreciation of the golden age of Happy Chef. Looking back now it's easy to see that the time in which this book was written truly was the Golden Age of Happy's influence and that things will never be so good again, but that shouldn't hinder the influence these teachings can still have on us today (Book 4:5).

Matt Bergstrom and Nathan Tolzmann
2015

The authors listen to the words of the Great Chef